Goddess Isis

AND THE ART OF MANIFESTATION

Ancient Egyptian Wisdom for Modern Creation

Goddess Isis and the Art of Manifestation: Ancient Egyptian Wisdom for Modern Creation

Welcome to the enchanting realm of Goddess Wisdom, where transformative books dedicated to goddesses from diverse cultures await you. Each captivating book delves into the essence of a distinct goddess, offering you the opportunity to embark on a profound journey of self-transformation. Immerse yourself in the captivating world of divine feminine archetypes such as Aphrodite, Athena, Queen Cleopatra, Isis, Kali, Lakshmi, Freya, Brigid, Amaterasu, Diana, and Inanna.

Also, within these sacred books, you will encounter the archetypes of Mother, Warrior, Trickster, Death and Underworld, Nature, as well as Love and Beauty. Drawing upon their timeless wisdom and practical guidance, you will uncover the remarkable potential they hold to inspire and empower you. Explore the nurturing energy exuded by the Mother Goddesses, tap into the indomitable strength of the Warrior Goddesses, embrace the whimsical playfulness of the Trickster Goddesses, courageously confront your fears alongside the Death and Underworld Goddesses, reconnect with the profound serenity of the Nature Goddesses, and discover the awe-inspiring beauty championed by the Love and Beauty Goddesses.

Allow yourself to be swept away by the transformative power of the goddesses as you embark on a personal journey of growth and empowerment. Unleash your true potential by immersing yourself in their timeless wisdom and harnessing their sacred energy. Together, let us awaken the divine within and forge a path of profound self-discovery and empowerment.

All of my books are available here
https://www.amazon.com/author/nicholemuir

www.nicholemuir.com

Facebook.com / Nichole Muir Goddess Wisdom

Contents

Chapter 1: Introduction to Goddess Isis and Manifestation

As we embark on this journey of understanding ancient wisdom and applying it in our lives, let's start by understanding the heart of this wisdom – the Egyptian goddess Isis, and the concept of manifestation.

Isis is one of the most important goddesses in ancient Egypt. Her name is derived from the ancient Egyptian word 'Iset', which means 'throne'. As the goddess of the throne, she was the symbol of pharaonic power. However, her power and influence stretched beyond more political authority. She was a figure of magic, motherhood, and healing. Through her myths and stories, Isis embodies the ability to overcome obstacles and create something meaningful out of chaos, making her an ideal guide for our exploration into manifestation.

Manifestation, in its simplest form, is the act of bringing something tangible into your life through belief and attraction. It could be anything from a new job, a better health, improved relationships, or even a sense of inner peace. The basic principle is that by imagining an idea, focusing your intent, and taking purposeful action, you can turn this idea into reality.

This concept of manifestation isn't new; it's been around for centuries. Ancient Egyptians believed in the power of words and thoughts. They practiced elaborate rituals, used symbols and amulets, and invoked their gods' help to manifest their desires. Isis, with her magic and wisdom, often played a central role in these practices.

In the modern world, manifestation has found its roots in the law of attraction, a philosophy suggesting that positive or negative thoughts bring positive or negative experiences. Despite the gap of centuries, the essence remains the same: our thoughts and intentions have the power to shape our reality.

Before we delve into this further, let's prepare ourselves with an opening meditation for grounding and focusing one's energy.

Meditation

Sit comfortably, your back straight, and close your eyes. Take a moment to become aware of your breathing. Don't rush this process; it's about settling down, gradually attuning to the natural rhythm of your breath. Feel the air enter your nostrils, filling your lungs, and then slowly leaving your body. Let this process anchor you in the present moment.

Now, visualize roots growing from your body, reaching down into the earth. Feel these roots drawing energy up into your body, grounding you, providing stability and balance. This is your connection to the earth, a reminder of your physical existence. Feel this energy spread through your body, from your toes all the way to the crown of your head.

Now, shift your attention to the sky above. Imagine a beam of light descending from the cosmos. This light represents divine energy, wisdom, and inspiration. Feel this light entering your body through the crown of your head and flowing down to meet the earth's energy in your heart.

Hold this image in your mind: the meeting of earth and cosmos within you. This is your center, a place of balance between the physical and the spiritual, the known and the unknown, the human and the divine.

Breathe in this energy, and as you exhale, let go of any tension, any worry, or negative thoughts. Feel them leaving your body, making room for calmness, clarity, and focus.

As you inhale, repeat silently to yourself: "I am open to receive." As you exhale, repeat: "I release what no longer serves me."

Stay with this cycle for a few minutes or as long as you feel comfortable.

When you're ready, slowly bring your awareness back to your physical surroundings. Open your eyes gently. Take a moment to thank yourself for dedicating this time to connect with your inner self.

This meditation serves as a starting point on our journey with Isis and the art of manifestation. As we progress through the chapters, we will explore more complex concepts, delve deeper into Isis's wisdom, and learn techniques that you can use to transform your life. It's a journey that requires an open mind, a willing heart, and the courage to confront and change deep-seated beliefs and patterns.

This isn't just about manifesting specific desires—it's about learning to navigate life with more intention and awareness. It's about understanding that we're active participants in shaping our reality. And most importantly, it's about realizing that, like Isis, we carry within us the magic and power to transform our world.

As we move forward, we'll learn to connect with Isis, work with symbols and amulets, harness the power of thoughts, practice affirmations, visualize success, perform rituals, and use nature and lunar cycles to our advantage. It's an exciting journey, and I invite you to embark on it with an open mind and heart.

By tapping into the wisdom of Isis, we can understand and utilize the power of manifestation to create a life that reflects our deepest desires and highest values. Remember, this is a personal journey, one that will look different for everyone. Be patient with yourself, trust in the process, and most importantly, enjoy the journey.

Welcome to the world of Isis and the Art of Manifestation.

Chapter 2: Who is Goddess Isis?

Goddess Isis is one of the most prominent goddesses in ancient Egyptian mythology, known for her role as a wife, mother, magician, and healer. Her worship was not confined to Egypt; it expanded throughout the Greco-Roman world until the decline of paganism.

Born to the sky goddess Nut and the earth god Geb, Isis was one of the earliest and most significant deities in ancient Egypt. She was part of the Heliopolitan Ennead, a family of nine deities that also included Osiris, Seth, and Nephthys.

Isis is often depicted with a throne-shaped glyph on her head, symbolizing her as the queen of the gods. She is also shown with wings, highlighting her role as a protective goddess. The hieroglyphs that spell her name can be translated as "she of the throne," representing her power and status within the pantheon of Egyptian gods.

Perhaps the most well-known story about Isis is her relationship with her brother and husband, Osiris. According to legend, Osiris was a benevolent king of Egypt, who was murdered by his envious brother Seth. Seth scattered Osiris's body parts across Egypt. Devastated by her husband's death, Isis embarked on a quest to find and reunite the scattered pieces.

With her magic, Isis brought Osiris back to life momentarily, enough to conceive their son, Horus. This event represents the first recorded resurrection in history, predating similar themes in other religions. Isis then raised Horus in secrecy to protect him from Seth, and he eventually grew up to avenge his father's death.

This poignant story exhibits Isis's unwavering dedication and love, making her an emblem of marital devotion and fidelity. It also highlights her role as a protective mother figure. Isis's tale of bringing Osiris back to life underscores her power as a magician and healer, and it is believed that her magical knowledge gave her a degree of power over all other gods.

Her connection to magic was so profound that ancient Egyptians believed she could control fate itself. They often invoked her during magical rites for protection against evil spirits, and her name was frequently called upon during spells in the Book of the Dead, an ancient Egyptian funerary text.

Isis was also revered as a compassionate goddess who listened to the prayers of the rich and poor alike. She was often approached by ordinary people seeking help with their problems, and she offered them protection and guidance.

Her temples were places of healing, where her priestesses and priests would perform healing rituals and spells. The sick would come from far and wide to be healed at these temples, further solidifying Isis's image as a healer.

In later periods, particularly during the Ptolemaic period and in the Roman Empire, the worship of Isis spread beyond the boundaries of Egypt. Temples dedicated to Isis were erected in various parts of the Greco-Roman world. Her image evolved during this tlme, absorhing traits from other goddesses, and she became associated with nature, agriculture, seafaring, and even lawmaking.

She was often seen as a universal goddess who encompassed all other goddesses. She was sometimes known as 'Isis of Ten Thousand Names', demonstrating her wide-ranging powers and characteristics.

In the Greco-Roman period, Isis was depicted in a Hellenized form, often shown as a woman wearing a long robe and a veil. A mural in Pompeii shows her holding a sistrum (a musical instrument) and a bucket, symbolizing her association with agriculture and the Nile's flooding.

Isis's cult did not just survive the advent of Christianity but continued to flourish well into the 6th century AD. However, with the rise of Christianity as the state religion of the Roman Empire, the temples of Isis were eventually closed. Yet, her legacy lived on, and her figure has since influenced the depiction of various Christian figures, particularly the Virgin Mary.

Even today, Isis continues to be a symbol of love, magic, healing, and power. Her story, which is filled with resilience and perseverance, continues to inspire, and her ancient wisdom is still relevant in the modern world. She embodies the strength and tenacity of the divine feminine and reminds us of the transformative power of love and dedication.

Understanding Isis and her many aspects is the first step towards aligning with her energy for manifestation. By delving into her stories, we can begin to understand the core aspects of her being and learn how to channel these aspects into our lives. This understanding provides a solid foundation for the chapters ahead as we journey deeper into the art of manifestation through the lens of Isis's ancient wisdom.

Chapter 3: Understanding Manifestation

Before we can delve into the intricacies of manifestation and how the ancient Egyptian goddess Isis fits into the picture, it is vital first to comprehend what manifestation truly is. We often hear the word in spiritual circles, especially in discussions around the law of attraction. But manifestation isn't just a new-age concept. It is a universal principle that underpins the fabric of our existence and has been recognized and harnessed by many ancient civilizations, including the Egyptians.

Manifestation, at its most basic level, is the process of turning thoughts, ideas, dreams, and desires into tangible reality. It is the act of creation - bringing forth something from nothing or transforming energy into matter. It's based on the understanding that everything in our universe is made of energy, vibrating at various frequencies. Our thoughts, emotions, and beliefs are also forms of energy. When we align our energetic vibration with what we desire, we attract it into our lives, thereby manifesting it.

The principle of manifestation is deeply rooted in the Hermetic philosophy of "As above, so below", which was central to ancient Egyptian spiritual teachings. This aphorism encapsulates the belief that the physical world is a mirror of the spiritual or celestial realm. Consequently, if we can imagine and align ourselves energetically with a desired outcome in our mind (above), we can manifest it in our physical reality (below).

Ancient Egyptians were proficient at harnessing the power of their minds. They understood that their thoughts were potent creative forces that could shape their reality. They used a combination of visualization, affirmations, sacred symbols, and ritual practices to impress their desires onto the cosmic mind or the divine creative force, personified in the pantheon of gods and goddesses, like Isis. This mystical act of impressing the cosmic mind, coupled with unwavering belief and expectancy, resulted in the manifestation of their desires in the material plane.

But why does manifestation matter? Why should we care about this seemingly mystical process? Manifestation matters because it empowers us. It teaches us that we are not passive observers of our lives, at the mercy of external forces. Instead, we are powerful creators who can shape our reality. This understanding can be transformative, bringing a deep sense of purpose, agency, and joy into our lives.

However, manifestation is not just about getting what we want. It's about aligning with our highest good, with the flow of life, and contributing to the collective good. It's about growth, learning, and realizing our potential. It's about becoming co-creators with the Universe or the Divine.

Manifestation involves much more than just thinking positive thoughts or visualizing our desires. While these are crucial elements, true manifestation requires aligning our thoughts, emotions, and actions. It requires us to embody the energy of our desires, to live as if they have already manifested.

Imagine you desire a loving, supportive relationship. If you just visualize this relationship but continue to harbor self-doubt, fear, and past emotional wounds within you, you're sending mixed signals to the Universe. Your thoughts are saying one thing, but your emotions and actions are saying another. However, if you nurture self-love, foster healing, and engage in activities that make you feel loved and supported, you're embodying the energy of your desire. You become an energetic match for that loving relationship, thereby drawing it to you.

Now that we have a basic understanding of what manifestation is, let's try a simple meditation to open our minds to the potential of manifestation.

Manifestation Meditation:

Begin by finding a quiet, comfortable place where you won't be disturbed. Sit in a comfortable position, close your eyes, and take a few deep breaths. With each exhale, let go of any tension or worry.

Now, visualize a golden ball of light in your heart center. This ball of light represents your creative potential, your ability to manifest. As you inhale, see this light expanding, growing brighter and larger. As you exhale, feel this light radiating outwards, filling your entire being.

Next, think of something small that you would like to manifest. It could be a day filled with joy, a positive interaction with a friend, or finding a lost item. Visualize this desire as clearly as you can within the golden light in your heart center.

Feel the joy and excitement of your desire already being fulfilled. Let this feeling fill your entire being, radiating outwards along with the golden light. Hold this visualization and feeling for a few moments.

Now, release the image of your desire and the associated feelings into the Universe, trusting that it will take care of the details. Visualize your desire floating away from you and dissolving into the Universe, knowing that what is yours will come to you.

Finish the meditation by taking a few more deep breaths, then slowly opening your eyes. Carry this feeling of trust and expectancy with you throughout your day.

This is a basic manifestation meditation to get you started. As we delve deeper into the wisdom of Isis and the ancient Egyptian practices, we will explore more complex and powerful manifestation techniques. Remember, manifestation is a journey of growth and discovery, not just a means to an end. Be open to the lessons along the way as you unlock your innate creative potential.

Chapter 4: The Role of Goddess Isis in Manifestation

Isis, a name that resonates with power, compassion, and the magic of creation, has been an influential deity in various cultures and times. Her roles are many - she is the goddess of motherhood, the guardian of children, the patron of nature and magic, and a guide to the underworld. However, it is her role as the goddess of creation and manifestation that we aim to understand and embody in this chapter.

In the cosmology of Ancient Egypt, Isis was known as the Divine Mother who gave birth to all of creation. She embodied the power of manifestation, not just as the bearer of life, but also as the originator of the metaphysical process by which thoughts and desires materialize into reality. This understanding of Isis can be leveraged to tap into the art of modern creation or manifestation.

To fully understand Isis's role in manifestation, we must delve into the ancient stories and myths that surround her. One such story tells of Isis gaining power over the sun god Ra. Isis, being a master of magic, created a serpent from the earth's dust and the spittle of Ra. This serpent bit Ra, creating an unbearable poison. Isis offered to heal Ra if he revealed his true name, a secret that held immense power. Finally, desperate for relief, Ra conceded. Upon learning his true name, Isis acquired unimaginable power, becoming a deity of creation, magic, and manifestation. This myth beautifully illustrates the key elements of the manifestation process: desire (Isis's wish for power), action (creating the serpent), and eventual realization (gaining power).

Ancient Egyptians believed that words held a creative force, and Isis's mastery over magic words was considered the basis of her manifestation power. This resonates with the modern understanding of affirmations in the process of manifestation. Affirmations, like the ancient magic words, when repeated with intention and belief, resonate with the universe's energy, attracting corresponding experiences and realities.

Isis is also associated with the 'Ankh,' the ancient Egyptian symbol of life, underscoring her profound connection to creation and manifestation. Often depicted carrying an Ankh, Isis is a reminder of the persistent flow of life force energy that we can tap into for manifestation.

Now, as we are beginning to grasp Isis's role in manifestation, let us perform a guided meditation to align ourselves with Isis's creative energy.

Close your eyes and take a deep, calming breath. Visualize yourself in the sacred land of ancient Egypt. As the sun begins to set, painting the sky with hues of red and gold, you see the magnificent River Nile flowing with gentle might.

Walk towards it, feeling the warm sand beneath your feet.

As you reach the river bank, you see a grand throne with the goddess Isis seated upon it, her emerald-green eyes meeting yours. She is adorned in a dress of gold and blue, a golden circlet on her head, and in her hand, she holds the Ankh, the symbol of life.

Feel her powerful, nurturing energy envelop you as you approach. Kneel before Isis and express your desire to understand the art of manifestation. Watch as she lifts the Ankh and points it towards you. A brilliant light emerges from the Ankh, washing over you, filling you with a profound sense of wisdom and power.

In this divine light, you feel a deep connection with the goddess. You understand the essence of Isis's power - the realization that you are a co-creator of your reality. Isis's story is not just an ancient myth; it is a metaphorical narrative of your personal power to manifest your deepest desires into reality.

Stay in this visualisation, basking in the energy of Isis, absorbing her wisdom, her power. Feel this connection to the divine fostering within you the strength to manifest your desires.

As you come out of this meditation, carry this feeling with you. Remember that manifestation, like Isis's magic, requires patience, intention, and belief in your intrinsic creative power. The divine essence of Isis now lives within you, guiding your way towards successful manifestation.

In the following chapters, we will delve deeper into the practicalities of manifestation. Drawing on Isis's wisdom, we will learn to use tools such as affirmations, sacred symbols, nature, and feminine power in the art of modern creation. Remember, the journey of manifestation is a journey of self-discovery. As we journey forward, let Isis be your guide, helping you unlock your true potential and create the reality you desire.

Chapter 5: Harnessing the Power of Thought

Throughout the ages, humans have sought to understand the mysteries of the mind and the immense power it holds over our lives. This is a concept not only recognized by modern psychologists but also by ancient spiritual traditions, including that of the Egyptians. According to these age-old beliefs, our thoughts not only shape our reality, they are reality.

The ancients believed in the 'law of correspondence,' succinctly stated as "as above, so below; as within, so without". This axiom is fundamental to the art of manifestation and central to the worship of Isis, the Egyptian goddess of magic and life.

Isis was the divine embodiment of the power of thoughts, often credited with the creation of all things through her incantations. She understood the power of words and thoughts, demonstrating that whatever was held within the mind could be reflected in the physical realm.

Harnessing the Power of Thought

Harnessing the power of thought is no less important in our lives today than it was in ancient Egypt. In fact, with our understanding of modern psychology and neuroscience, we have come to recognize this as a fundamental truth: our thoughts and perceptions shape our reality.

Consider the vast capacity of the human mind, filled with limitless thoughts and ideas. It is an entity that constantly shapes our actions, emotions, and, eventually, our reality. Every thought you think, every belief you hold, changes the way you experience and interact with the world.

Imagine your thoughts as seeds. If you plant seeds of fear, doubt, and negativity, you create a reality that mirrors these qualities. On the other hand, if you plant seeds of love, positivity, and abundance, you set the stage for a reality reflecting these attributes.

For us to harness the power of thought in our favor, we must first become aware of the nature of our thoughts and intentionally direct them towards the reality we wish to create.

Practical Steps to Harness the Power of Thought

Thought Awareness: The first step in harnessing the power of thought is to become aware of your thoughts. Pay attention to what you are thinking and how those thoughts make you feel. If you find that your thoughts are predominantly negative, intentionally try to shift your focus to more positive thoughts.

Positive Affirmations: Once you have become aware of your thoughts, you can begin to shape them consciously. One of the best ways to do this is through the use of positive affirmations. Affirmations are short, powerful statements that you say to yourself in the present tense, which help to shape your reality. For instance, instead of thinking, "I can't do this," try affirming, "I am capable and confident."

Visualization: Another powerful tool in harnessing the power of thought is visualization. This involves creating a mental image of the outcome you desire. The more vivid and detailed the visualization, the more potent it becomes. You could visualize being in perfect health, having a loving relationship, or achieving a professional goal.

Belief: Belief is a potent form of thought. When you truly believe in something, your thoughts align with that belief, and you become more likely to manifest it. It's not enough to merely say or visualize your desires—you must believe in their possibility.

Meditation for Harnessing the Power of Thought

Now, let's practice a simple yet powerful meditation that will help you harness the power of thought. Find a quiet, peaceful place where you won't be disturbed. Sit comfortably, close your eyes, and take a few deep, cleansing breaths.

Grounding: Start by visualizing roots growing from the soles of your feet, penetrating deep into the earth. Feel the stability and strength this connection to the earth provides you.

Centering: Now, imagine a beam of light entering through the crown of your head and filling your entire being. Feel this light centering your mind, calming your thoughts, and aligning you with your inner wisdom.

Thought Awareness: Spend a few moments observing your thoughts. Don't try to change or judge them, just observe. Notice if they are positive or negative, helpful or unhelpful.

Thought Transformation: Begin to transform any negative thoughts into positive ones. If you notice a thought like, "I'm not good enough," change it to, "I am worthy and capable." Do this for as many thoughts as you can.

Visualization: Now, visualize a scenario in which your transformed thoughts are your reality. If you've transformed the thought, "I'm not successful," to, "I am successful," visualize what that success looks like.

Belief: Spend a few moments in this visualization and allow the feeling of belief to build. Trust that this reality is not only possible but already unfolding.

Gratitude: Finally, express gratitude for your ability to shape your reality through the power of thought. Gratitude serves as an affirmation of the abundance already present In your life.

Closing: When you feel ready, bring your awareness back to your physical surroundings. Take a few more deep breaths, and then gently open your eyes.

By harnessing the power of thought, we align ourselves with the wisdom of Isis and the potent practice of manifestation. Remember, each thought is a seed that can grow into a reality. Therefore, let's choose our thoughts wisely, cultivating those that reflect the reality we desire.

Chapter 6: Sacred Symbols and Amulets

In our exploration of Isis and the art of manifestation, it is critical to delve into one of the essential aspects of ancient Egyptian culture: the use of sacred symbols and amulets. Just as words were believed to carry power in ancient Egyptian cosmology, symbols too held a potent spiritual significance. They were viewed not just as mere representations but as living entities embodying the energies and attributes they symbolized. Among these, several are closely associated with

Isis, making them invaluable in our journey towards mastering the art of manifestation.

One of the primary symbols associated with Isis is the 'Tyet,' also known as the 'Isis Knot' or 'Blood of Isis.' This symbol, often made of red jasper or carnelian, resembles an ankh but with the arms curved down. It was believed to possess protective properties, especially for the dead, and was frequently depicted on funerary equipment. To the ancient Egyptians, the 'Blood of Isis' was symbolic of divine, renewing life force and magic, crucial aspects of manifestation. By aligning ourselves with the energy of the Tyet, we connect to Isis's nurturing and protective energies, thus creating a safe space for our intentions to manifest.

Another significant symbol is the 'throne' hieroglyph, representative of Isis's name itself, meaning 'throne' or 'seat.' In ancient Egyptian belief, the throne was more than just a piece of furniture; it was a symbol of power, authority, and legitimacy. By focusing on this symbol, we can tap into the energy of personal power and leadership, essential qualities when manifesting our desired reality.

The 'winged Isis' symbol, which depicts the goddess with outstretched wings, is a powerful representation of her role as a protector and nurturer. Her wings were said to provide shelter and safety while also offering the promise of renewal and rebirth, similar to a phoenix rising from the ashes. This symbol serves as a reminder that, like Isis, we have the power to rise above our challenges and manifest our desired outcomes.

Amulets, like symbols, were fundamental to ancient Egyptian spiritual practices. Often, these small pieces of jewelry or inscriptions were worn for protection or to confer certain attributes upon the wearer.

The 'Isis knot' amulet, a physical representation of the Tyet symbol, was frequently worn for protection and to harness the regenerative power of Isis. Holding or wearing such an amulet during our manifestation meditations can help amplify our intentions and connect us more deeply with Isis's energy.

Similarly, the 'ankh,' an amulet and a hieroglyph meaning 'life,' was closely associated with Isis, who is often depicted holding an ankh. The ankh embodies the concept of eternal life, and its key-like shape has led to interpretations associating it with unlocking the gates of the afterlife. However, in the context of manifestation, we can view the ankh as a key to unlocking the life we desire.

Working with these symbols and amulets in our manifestation practice can significantly enhance our connection with Isis and the qualities she embodies.

Now, let's move into the meditative practice for this chapter. Before you begin, it would be beneficial to have an image or representation of the Isis Knot, the throne hieroglyph, and the winged Isis. If you have Isis Knot or ankh amulets, have them close.

Find a quiet space where you won't be disturbed. Begin by grounding yourself. Feel your feet firmly planted on the earth, and visualize roots extending from your soles, anchoring you to the ground. Take a deep breath in, hold for a moment, then exhale fully. Repeat this breathing cycle a few times until you feel calm and centered.

Hold the image or representation of the Isis Knot in your mind's eye, or gaze upon it if you have a physical representation. Feel its protective energy enveloping you, creating a safe space for your manifestation. Imagine this energy as a vibrant red light, warm and nurturing.

Next, turn your focus to the throne hieroglyph. Feel its energy of authority and power pulsating. Picture this energy as a brilliant golden light, radiating from the symbol and filling you with confidence and assertiveness.

Finally, connect with the energy of the winged Isis. Picture her wings outstretched, sheltering you, offering protection and nurturing. Feel this energy as a brilliant white light, gently touching and healing all parts of you, infusing you with a sense of rebirth and renewal.

Now, if you have an Isis Knot or ankh amulet, hold it in your hand. Feel its weight, texture, and temperature. As you breathe in, imagine your breath carrying your intention into the amulet. As you breathe out, visualize the amulet glowing brighter with your intention. If you don't have an amulet, visualize holding one in your mind's eye and follow the same process.

Spend as long as you feel necessary in this meditation, continuing to breathe in your intentions and breathe out into the amulet. When you feel ready, gently bring your awareness back to the room. Open your eyes if they were closed.

Know that the energies of these symbols, and of Isis, are with you, nurturing and protecting your intentions as they manifest into reality. Carry your charged amulet with you, or keep it in a sacred space, as a physical reminder of these energies and your manifestation intentions.

The sacred symbols and amulets of Isis offer a powerful way to connect with her energies and the ancient wisdom she embodies. By integrating these into our manifestation practice, we create a bridge between the ancient world and our modern lives, between the physical and spiritual, and between intention and manifestation. Remember, the power of Isis is within you, waiting to be unlocked and harnessed for your creation.

Chapter 7: The Role of Affirmations

Affirmations have long been recognized as a powerful tool in the manifestation process. In this chapter, we will delve into the concept of affirmations from the perspective of ancient Egyptian wisdom and the goddess Isis, and how they can be incorporated into our modern manifestation practices.

What are affirmations? Simply put, affirmations are positive statements that can help you to challenge and overcome self-sabotaging and negative thoughts. They are typically in the present tense and aim to reinforce belief in one's abilities, values, and worth. Affirmations are designed to alter the subconscious mind, transforming our thoughts, feelings, and ultimately, our reality.

Why are affirmations so important in the manifestation process? The answer lies in understanding our mind's function. We know the mind is divided into the conscious and the subconscious. The subconscious mind is like fertile soil, absorbing everything planted in it, whether good or bad. It is in this fertile soil of our mind that we plant the seeds of our reality, our affirmations.

When we repeatedly affirm something, we are planting seeds of belief in our subconscious. These seeds then grow, blossoming into our reality. This principle aligns with the ancient Egyptian understanding of creation, where spoken words held immense power. Their gods and goddesses created the universe through their voices, bringing things into existence through the spoken word. Isis, in particular, was famed for her magical incantations and was regarded as one of the most potent deities in this respect.

From Isis, we learn the power of affirmations as a divine feminine practice. In her mythology, Isis used her power of affirmation and incantation to resurrect her husband Osiris, proving that words can breathe life into our desires and intentions. Her wisdom teaches us that we too, like Isis, can use our words to breathe life into our reality, to manifest our desires.

To incorporate affirmations into our manifestation practices, we first need to define our intentions clearly. What is it that you desire? What do you want to manifest? Once you have your intention, craft an affirmation that aligns with this intention. Remember to keep your affirmation in the present tense, positive, and personal. It should resonate with you at a deep, personal level.

For instance, if your intention is to attract abundance, your affirmation could be: "I am a magnet for prosperity and abundance flows effortlessly into my life." If you're seeking love, you could affirm: "I am love, and I attract loving and caring relationships into my life."

Once you have crafted your affirmation, the next step is to introduce it into your subconscious mind. This step requires practice, repetition, and consistency. Repeat your affirmations daily, preferably in the morning when you wake up and at night before you sleep. These are the times when your subconscious mind is the most receptive.

For a deeper integration of the affirmations, couple them with a meditative practice. This practice helps to quiet the mind, making it more receptive to the affirmations, and allowing them to penetrate deeper into the subconscious.

Isis Affirmation Meditation:

Find a quiet and comfortable space where you won't be disturbed. Sit comfortably, with your back straight. Close your eyes and take a few deep breaths.

Visualize the goddess Isis before you, her wings spread wide in protection and love. Feel her divine feminine energy surrounding you, nurturing you.

Once you feel calm and grounded, repeat your affirmation aloud or silently in your mind. As you do, visualize your affirmation as a seed you are planting in the fertile soil of your subconscious mind.

As you repeat your affirmation, visualize the seed sprouting, growing, and blossoming. See your affirmation manifesting as your reality. Feel the emotions that come with the manifestation of your desires.

Repeat this process for a few minutes, allowing the affirmation to integrate into your subconscious mind deeply.

When you're ready, thank Isis for her guidance and gently come back to your physical surroundings. Open your eyes, knowing your affirmation is already at work, creating your desired reality.

Incorporating the wisdom of Isis and the ancient Egyptians, affirmations can become a powerful tool in your manifestation toolkit. They can help to transform your thoughts, your beliefs, and ultimately, your reality. Remember, like Isis, your words hold the power to create. So, choose them wisely, speak them confidently, and manifest your desires into reality.

Chapter 8: Goddess Isis and the Cycle of Life

Understanding the full spectrum of life and death is integral to grasping the essence of manifestation. Ancient Egyptian religion was deeply entwined with the cycles of life, death, and rebirth, with goddess Isis playing a significant role in this cosmic dance. She was revered as the divine mother, nurturer, and the bringer of life, while also being closely associated with the mystery of death and the promise of rebirth. By comprehending these cycles, we can enhance our manifestation skills, for every end is a new beginning, every failure a stepping-stone to success, and every death a portal to rebirth.

Life, according to ancient Egyptian philosophy, was a journey of the soul, constantly evolving, learning, and manifesting its desires. The goddess Isis, with her unyielding resilience and creative power, epitomizes this journey. She has an innate capacity to transform, regenerate, and renew. Recognizing this pattern in our own lives can empower us to transcend our limitations, manifesting the best version of ourselves in every rebirth, whether it's a change in career, relationship, or personal development.

To begin, let us dive into the story of Isis and her husband Osiris. The tale of Isis resurrecting Osiris from death has been a central theme in ancient Egyptian mythology. It speaks volumes about the power of love, the magic of renewal, and the possibility of rebirth even in the direst of circumstances. Isis's determination in gathering the scattered pieces of Osiris's body, reviving him, and conceiving their son Horus, signifies the potency of rebirth and the cyclic nature of existence.

Isis's trials taught her that every phase of life, whether it's the bliss of birth or the agony of death, is essential in the grand scheme of existence. Each phase has its energy, and learning to channel these energies can open doors to potent manifestation.

Understanding the Birth Phase

The birth phase symbolizes the beginning of a cycle. It's the stage of new ideas, opportunities, and fresh starts. Here, the energy is vibrant and full of potential. Isis, as the Divine Mother, symbolizes this birthing energy. When you conceive a new idea or set a new intention, you engage with this birth energy.

For effective manifestation, it's crucial to nourish this energy, just like a mother would nurture her newborn. Meditation, visualization, and affirmative action can serve as sustenance for your goals, nurturing them from mere intentions to tangible outcomes.

Understanding the Life Phase

Life represents the phase of growth and evolution, an opportunity to learn, experience, and manifest our desires. Life is not a static phase; it's full of ups and downs, trials and triumphs. By embodying the perseverance of Isis, we can navigate through life's challenges, learning, and growing with every experience, thus bringing us closer to our manifestations.

Understanding the Death Phase

Often, the concept of death is associated with fear and loss. But in the wisdom of ancient Egypt, death is not the end but a transition. It's the phase of letting go, shedding the old to make way for the new. The story of Isis and Osiris teaches us that death can be a starting point for a new journey, a pathway to rebirth.

When it comes to manifestation, understanding the death phase is crucial. It teaches us to let go of outdated beliefs, past failures, or anything that no longer serves our purpose. This release makes space for new possibilities and brings us a step closer to our desired outcomes.

Understanding the Rebirth Phase

Rebirth is the resurrection from the ashes, the dawn after the darkest hour. It symbolizes hope, renewal, and transformation. Isis's act of bringing Osiris back to life is a testament to the power of rebirth. Rebirth holds the promise of a fresh start and new opportunities. It's the phase where the magic of manifestation unfolds, turning our intentions into reality.

Now that we've explored these cycles let's connect with them on a deeper level. This following guided meditation is designed to help you align with the cycles of birth, life, death, and rebirth for empowered manifestation.

Start by finding a quiet space where you won't be disturbed. Sit comfortably, close your eyes, and take a few deep breaths to ground yourself. Visualize yourself as a lotus seed buried deep in the mud at the bottom of a pond. This is the birth phase. With every breath, feel the potential within you, just like the potential within the seed.

As you inhale, imagine yourself breaking through the seed and beginning to grow towards the surface. This is the life phase. Feel the challenges as you push through the mud and the triumph as you break through the water to reach the surface.

Once you've reached the surface, visualize the lotus flower wilting and dying, its petals falling back into the water. This is the death phase. Embrace the process of letting go, surrendering to the flow of life.

Finally, envision a new lotus flower blooming from the old one's remains, beautiful and vibrant. This is the rebirth phase. Feel the joy and vitality of new beginnings. Stay in this phase for a while, savoring the energy of renewal.

Slowly come back to your breath and then to your physical presence. Open your eyes when you feel ready.

This meditation can be practiced as often as you like, serving as a reminder of the eternal cycles of life and death. The more we align with these cycles, the more we can harness their energies for manifestation. Just as Isis did, we can turn our trials into triumphs, our ends into beginnings, and manifest our deepest desires into reality.

Chapter 9: The Power of Visualization

Visualization is a potent tool for manifestation. It helps us shift from mere desire to active creation by bringing our goals into a vivid, multisensory reality within our mind. In this chapter, we will delve into how to use this ancient practice effectively, drawing inspiration from the time-tested wisdom of Isis and Ancient Egypt.

Isis was known as the mother of all creation in Ancient Egypt. Her mythology provides a powerful example of the art of visualization in action. When her husband, Osiris, was killed and dismembered,

Isis did not simply wish for his resurrection; she vividly imagined it, and she moved through the world, gathering his parts and bringing them together again, fully visualizing his revival. This story gives us an illustration of how our visions can be transformed into reality, using the power of our minds, our actions, and our determination.

Let's start by understanding visualization.

Understanding Visualization

Visualization is the mental technique of creating a picture or scenario in your mind, using as many senses as possible. The idea is to create a mental rehearsal or blueprint of what you want to manifest.

Science supports the efficacy of visualization. Studies show that the brain does not differentiate between a vividly imagined event and a real one. That's why athletes, performers, and successful business people often use visualization techniques to improve performance and achieve their goals.

In the context of manifestation, visualization serves two primary purposes: it clarifies your desires and aligns your subconscious mind with the outcome you want, making you more likely to take actions that lead to the manifestation of your goal.

Isis and Visualization

Isis herself was a master of visualization. As a goddess of magic, she knew the power of imagination coupled with intent. By seeing and feeling the reality she desired, she could bring it into existence. In essence, she created her reality through the images she formed and the feelings she invoked.

Isis teaches us that visualization is not merely a mental exercise. It involves our emotions, our senses, our intentions, and our actions. When we visualize, we are not just daydreaming. We are participating in the act of creation, channeling the goddess's energy into our intentions.

How to Practice Visualization

To practice visualization, start by finding a quiet place where you won't be disturbed. Sit comfortably, close your eyes, and take a few deep breaths to center yourself.

Next, think about what you want to manifest. Be as specific as possible. If it's a new job, imagine every detail of that job: the office, your colleagues, the work you're doing. If it's a relationship, visualize the person you want to be with, your interactions, the feelings of love and companionship.

Engage all your senses in the process. What can you see? What can you hear? What can you feel, taste, and smell? The more detailed your visualization, the more real it becomes to your mind.

Pay special attention to the feelings your visualization evokes. The emotional component is a crucial part of the process. Feel the joy, the satisfaction, the love, the excitement—whatever emotions your manifestation would bring.

As you visualize, believe in its reality. This is where the power of Isis comes in. Remember that she did not just see Osiris's resurrection; she fully believed in it, and so it happened. In the same way, trust that your visualization is not just a fantasy. It is a reality taking shape.

A Guided Isis Visualization Meditation

To aid you in your practice, here is a guided visualization meditation invoking the goddess Isis:

Start by getting into a comfortable position, close your eyes and take a few deep breaths. Feel your body relax with each exhale.

Invoke the presence of Isis by imagining her standing before you, radiating divine, warm light. Feel her energy filling the space around you.

Now, bring to mind what you want to manifest. See it as clearly as you can in your mind's eye.

Imagine Isis extending her hands towards you, and from her hands, visualize a radiant golden light flowing towards you.

Visualize this golden light enveloping you and creating a bubble around you. This is your safe, sacred space for creation.

Within this bubble, bring your visualization into greater detail. Make it as vivid as you can, engaging all your senses. If it's a physical object, visualize it from all angles. If it's a situation, imagine yourself in the midst of it.

Now, let the emotions flow. How do you feel having achieved your goal? Let the feelings fill you up. Feel the joy, the satisfaction, the peace.

As you dwell in this visualization, allow the energy of Isis to infuse it, enhancing its vibrancy and reality. Let her magic breathe life into your vision.

Stay with this scene as long as you like. Feel it, believe in it, know that it is real.

When you're ready, bring your focus back to your breath. Feel yourself grounded in the present moment, carrying your visualization within you.

Thank Isis for her presence and help, and when you feel ready, slowly open your eyes.

Repeat this meditation daily, and remember: you are not just visualizing your desire; you are creating it. Like Isis, you hold the power of creation within you.

The Journey Ahead

Remember, visualization is a practice. It becomes more potent with time. Just as Isis gathered the pieces of Osiris over time, your visions and manifestations will also gather shape and substance as you continually dedicate yourself to the practice.

Isis's wisdom teaches us that our visions can be molded into reality when we believe in them and align our actions towards them. Through visualization, we invoke the power of Isis, affirming our innate ability to create the life we desire.

So, engage your mind, embrace your senses, kindle your emotions, and step into the sacred space of creation. Your journey into the art of manifestation is well underway.

Chapter 10: Goddess Isis and Nature

Goddess Isis, the goddess of life, magic, and healing, held a profound association with nature in ancient Egyptian mythology. She was seen as the personification of the earth and its cycles, imbuing the environment around her with an essential, life-giving energy. This divine association provides an abundance of wisdom and techniques that we can draw upon to enhance our modern manifestation practices.

In today's era of digital technology and urbanized living, we often feel disconnected from the natural world. Yet, nature offers a profound source of energy, healing, and creative inspiration that can greatly enhance our manifestation practices. Isis's association with nature teaches us that by reconnecting with the natural world, we can tap into the primal rhythms of life and align our manifestation efforts with these powerful forces.

To begin exploring Isis's connection to nature and how it can aid in your manifestation journey, let's start with a grounding meditation. This meditation will help you reconnect with the earth and align your energy with its natural rhythms.

Find a quiet place where you can sit comfortably without disturbances. If you can, try to find a spot outdoors where you can directly touch the earth.

Close your eyes and take a few deep breaths. With each exhale, let go of any tension or worries.

Imagine your body as a tree, your feet as the roots digging deep into the earth, and your head reaching for the sky. Feel the energy from the earth nourishing your roots and the sunlight feeding your branches and leaves.

As you visualize this, invite Isis into your meditation by silently calling her name or visualizing her image. Ask her to help you connect with the earth's energy and align it with your own.

Spend a few minutes or as long as you need in this state, feeling the grounding energy of the earth and the nurturing energy of Isis. When you feel ready, gently bring your awareness back to your physical surroundings and open your eyes.

This meditation is a simple yet powerful way to reconnect with nature and harness its energy for your manifestation work.

Isis's association with nature is not limited to the earth alone. She was also considered a goddess of the sky and the sea. Her husband, Osiris, was the god of vegetation, and their son, Horus, was the god of the sky. These connections offer us a complete cycle of nature – earth, water, and sky, representing various aspects of natural life. These elements can be incorporated into our manifestation work to create a balanced and holistic approach.

The earth represents the material world, the tangible results we desire from our manifestation work. By connecting with the earth's energy, we ground our intentions in reality and give them a form to take shape. This grounding is crucial for successful manifestation.

Water, associated with the sea and river Nile in Isis's mythology, symbolizes the emotional and intuitive aspects of our lives. By attuning ourselves with the energy of water, we can tap into our feelings and intuition, vital tools in manifestation.

The sky symbolizes thought, inspiration, and spiritual connection. By connecting with sky energy, we open ourselves to divine guidance and expand our perceptions. This can help us see new possibilities and align our intentions with the higher good.

To apply this understanding of earth, water, and sky in your manifestation practices, you might consider creating rituals that honor these elements. For instance, you could perform your manifestation practices in a garden or park to connect with the earth's energy, near a body of water to tap into your emotional realm, or under the open sky to draw inspiration and spiritual guidance.

Goddess Isis's profound connection with nature offers an enriching dimension to our modern manifestation practices. By tapping into the earth's grounding energy, the emotional depths of water, and the expansive inspiration of the sky, we can align our manifestation work with the primal rhythms of nature. As you continue your journey of manifestation, remember to honor and connect with these natural forces, for they are a potent source of magic, power, and life.

Chapter 11: Rituals for Manifestation

Manifestation is not a product of modern mysticism or New Age thought alone. It is, in fact, a practice that is as old as humanity itself, and the Ancient Egyptians were no strangers to it. In fact, they used various rituals to harness the power of the universe, many of which were dedicated to the goddess Isis.

Rituals create an avenue to channel our energies and intentions, enhancing our connection with the spiritual world and Isis, the goddess of fertility, magic, and creation. This chapter will guide you on how to perform specific rituals for effective manifestation, inspired by Isis's wisdom and might. Each ritual will be coupled with a preparatory meditation, helping you to center and focus your intentions and energies.

Let's start by understanding the core purpose of rituals in manifestation.

The Purpose of Rituals in Manifestation

Rituals are an integral part of many spiritual practices. They offer a structured way to express our intentions, provide a physical enactment of our desires, and establish a stronger bond with the spiritual forces at work.

In the context of manifestation, rituals serve several key purposes:

Clarifying Intentions: Rituals compel us to be clear about our desires, turning vague wishes into concrete goals.

Focusing Energy: They allow us to gather and concentrate our energy on what we wish to manifest.

Establishing Connection: Rituals can connect us with the universal energy, higher beings, and in this context, Isis, amplifying our manifestation potential.

Grounding Intentions in Reality: By creating a physical representation of our intentions, rituals help bridge the gap between the spiritual and physical realms.

Now that we understand the purpose and power of rituals let's dive into the practical aspect of performing manifestation rituals inspired by Isis.

Preparing for the Ritual

Before you embark on any ritual, it is crucial to prepare yourself and your space adequately. This preparation aids in creating a sacred space that fosters positive energy and focuses intention. The preparatory steps include:

Clear Your Space: Ensure the area you choose for your ritual is clean and free from clutter. You might want to consider smudging with sage or using sound from bells or singing bowls to cleanse the area energetically.

Gather Your Tools: Depending on the specific ritual, you may need different tools, such as candles, crystals, a representation of Isis, a bowl of water, or pen and paper. Have these ready before you begin.

Ground Yourself: Perform a grounding meditation to center your energy and focus. Close your eyes and take deep breaths, visualizing your connection with the Earth.

Isis Ritual for Manifestation

For the Isis Ritual for Manifestation, you will need a candle, a representation of Isis (such as a statue, amulet, or picture), a small piece of paper, and a pen.

Set the Space: Place your Isis representation in a prominent place. Light the candle, representing the light of Isis.

Meditate: Close your eyes and focus on your breath. Visualize the light of the candle radiating the warm, nurturing energy of Isis around you.

State Your Intention: Think about what you wish to manifest. Be clear and concise, focusing on positive outcomes. Once you have your intention in mind, write it on the piece of paper.

Invoke Isis: With your eyes closed, hold the paper with your intention written on it and say, "Great Isis, Goddess of Creation and Magic, I invoke your presence and ask for your guidance and assistance. May this desire, grounded in love and harmlessness, manifest in the highest good for all."

Visualize Your Desire: Spend some time visualizing your desire as already manifested. Feel the joy and gratitude, invoking as much emotion as possible.

Release the Intention: Burn the piece of paper in the candle's flame (be careful to ensure safety). As the paper burns, imagine your intention being released to Isis and the Universe.

Close the Ritual: Thank Isis for her guidance and assistance. Extinguish the candle, symbolizing the completion of the ritual.

Remember, the most important aspect of any ritual is your intention and focus. The tools and actions are merely aids in directing your energy and intent. As you become comfortable with ritual work, feel free to adapt the procedures to better suit your personal beliefs and needs.

Rituals provide a tangible way to connect with the powerful energy of Isis and the universe. By performing these rituals with clear intent and a focused mind, you can harness this power to manifest your desires. As you continue your practice, remember that manifestation is not just about creating what you want but aligning with the highest good for yourself and all beings. Happy manifesting!

Chapter 12: Harnessing Lunar Energy

Goddess Isis, the revered goddess of ancient Egypt, is a multifaceted deity with various symbols and associations that reflect her vast powers and characteristics. One such association is with the Moon - a celestial body of great importance to the Egyptians. The connection between Isis and the moon is not only mystical and beautiful but also holds profound implications for the art of manifestation.

In Egyptian hieroglyphs, the image of Isis is often seen with a moon disk nestled between her cow horns, symbolizing her dominion over the night and her power to control the tides of life. By understanding and embodying Isis's lunar connections, we can leverage this powerful association to enhance our manifestation efforts. This chapter seeks to elaborate on how we can align our intentions and actions with the moon's phases in a way that resonates with Isis's ancient wisdom.

It is essential first to understand the moon's significance and its various phases. The moon's cycle is a cycle of growth and decline, symbolic of life's ebb and flow. This cycle is divided into four main phases: the New Moon, the First Quarter Moon, the Full Moon, and the Last Quarter Moon. Each phase carries its unique energy and symbolism, which, when harnessed correctly, can significantly bolster the manifestation process.

The New Moon is a time of beginnings, akin to planting a seed. In terms of manifestation, the New Moon offers a potent time to set new intentions, start projects, and sow the seeds of our dreams. Just as Isis resurrected her husband Osiris, we too can use the New Moon's energy to bring our desires to life.

The First Quarter Moon signifies a time of action and challenges. It is during this phase that we must take the necessary steps towards manifesting our desires, even in the face of adversity. Like Isis, who faced countless obstacles with resilience, we are encouraged to persist in our endeavors, undeterred by any hurdles we encounter.

The Full Moon is the climax of the lunar cycle, a time of fruition and realization. Here, the intentions set during the New Moon have the potential to manifest fully. The Full Moon is a time of celebration and gratitude. As we rejoice in the realization of our desires, we invoke the blessings of Isis, thanking her for guiding us in our manifestation journey.

The Last Quarter Moon is a time of release and introspection. Just as Isis had her moments of retreat and reflection, this phase urges us to let go of what no longer serves us and introspect on our journey thus far. It is a time for cleansing, healing, and preparing for a new manifestation cycle.

Now that we understand the moon's phases, it is crucial to learn how to harness this energy for manifestation. It starts by synchronizing our intentions with the moon's cycle. During the New

Moon, take some time to meditate and clearly define what you wish to manifest. Write down your intentions and visualize them coming to life.

As the moon moves into its First Quarter phase, spring into action. Identify the steps you need to take towards your goals and execute them. Like Isis, face your challenges with courage and resilience. Keep your intentions in mind, and remember that each step brings you closer to your goals.

When the Full Moon arrives, it's time to celebrate and give thanks. Create a small ritual of gratitude, acknowledging your accomplishments and thanking Isis for her guidance. This ritual can be as simple as lighting a candle, enjoying a meal, or dancing under the moonlight. The key is to feel joy and gratitude in your heart.

Finally, when the Last Quarter Moon comes, reflect on your journey and release what no longer serves you. This release can take many forms – it can be a habit, a thought pattern, or anything that hinders your growth. By letting go, you create space for new desires and goals to take root in the next lunar cycle.

As we align our actions with the lunar cycle, we are not merely observing celestial events; we are consciously participating in the universal ebb and flow of life – a flow that Isis herself embodies.

Now, let's move onto a lunar meditation designed to align us with the moon's energies and Isis's lunar essence.

Sit comfortably and take a few deep breaths. Visualize the moon in your mind's eye, see its luminous glow. Now imagine Isis, with her moon disk, standing against the night sky. Feel her powerful yet nurturing presence surrounding you. As you breathe in, draw in the energy of the moon and Isis into your being, filling you with a radiant glow. As you breathe out, release any barriers to your manifestation goals.

As you sync your breath with this visualization, set your intentions. If it's a New Moon, focus on what you wish to manifest. If it's the First Quarter Moon, focus on the actions needed to fulfill your desires. During the Full Moon, fill your heart with gratitude, and during the Last Quarter Moon, release what no longer serves you.

Continue this meditation for as long as you feel necessary. When you're ready, slowly bring your awareness back to the physical world. Remember, just like the moon that waxes and wanes, our lives also undergo cycles of ebb and flow. By aligning ourselves with these cycles and invoking the lunar energy of Isis, we can powerfully enhance our manifestation efforts.

Goddess Isis's association with the moon provides us with a potent pathway to enhance our manifestation capabilities. By understanding the lunar phases and their energies, aligning our actions with these phases, and utilizing lunar meditation, we harness an ancient wisdom that can significantly bolster our manifestation endeavors. So, as you navigate your journey of creation, remember the moon, remember Isis, and remember the power they hold for your manifestation success.

Chapter 13: Isis and Feminine Power

One of the most profound aspects of Isis, the ancient Egyptian goddess, is her embodiment of divine feminine power. Isis, revered as the 'Goddess of Life,' is an epitome of strength, intuition, healing, and creation. Understanding the essence of Isis and the feminine power she radiates opens up the opportunity to manifest our desires by aligning with her energy. In this chapter, we will delve into Isis's symbol as a figure of feminine power, discussing the role of feminine energy in manifestation, and introducing a meditation to tap into the divine feminine.

The Divine Feminine: An Understanding

Often depicted with a throne as her headdress and wings by her side, Isis personifies the aspects of nurturing, protection, healing, wisdom, and creation, quintessential to the divine feminine. To comprehend this, we must first understand the concept of the divine feminine.

The divine feminine is an energy that permeates the universe. It is a universal force that resides within everyone, regardless of gender. It's associated with qualities like intuition, compassion, emotional understanding, creativity, and nurturing. Tapping into this energy helps balance the often overly masculine, action-driven society, creating harmony and promoting the manifestation process.

Isis: An Embodiment of the Divine Feminine

Isis, known for her immense wisdom, nurturing nature, and the ability to create and heal, epitomizes the divine feminine. As a mother, she symbolizes nurturing and caring. As a wife, she demonstrates loyalty and commitment. Her wisdom and magic are testaments to her inner strength and determination. These qualities are not only a representation of Isis as a divine being but also indicative of the feminine power within us that we can harness.

The strength of Isis was demonstrated when she brought her husband Osiris back to life, signifying regeneration and healing. This anecdote of Isis reflects the resilience and determination intrinsic to feminine energy. The creative power of Isis, another prominent attribute, is depicted in the myths where she breathed life into her son, Horus. This shows her role as a life-giver, a creator, again underscoring the might of the feminine.

Feminine Power and Manifestation

The process of manifestation aligns perfectly with feminine energy, and Isis provides a blueprint to follow. Just as Isis created life, we create our realities. Manifestation involves visualization, creativity, nurturing our intentions, and patiently allowing them to unfold - all of these are aspects of feminine power.

The act of creation is inherently feminine. The process requires nurturing an idea, much like a mother nurtures a child. It's about intuitively connecting with your desires and transforming them from the ethereal to the tangible realm.

Moreover, the feminine power is also about resilience. We may not always manifest what we desire at the first attempt. It's during these times that the resilience of feminine power, as shown by Isis, helps us to persevere.

Guided Meditation: Connecting with Isis and the Divine Feminine

Let's now engage in a meditation practice to connect with Isis's divine feminine energy. This meditation is intended to tap into your inherent feminine power and use it to amplify your manifestation abilities.

Begin by finding a comfortable position where you won't be disturbed. Close your eyes and take a few deep breaths, grounding yourself in the present moment.

Visualize yourself in an ancient Egyptian temple, the temple of Isis. The sandstone walls are adorned with hieroglyphics, narrating tales of power, resilience, and creation. In the center stands a grand statue of Isis, resplendent with her wings spread out and a throne on her head.

Approach the statue and stand before it. Take a moment to feel her energy, nurturing and powerful. Now, visualize a soft, golden light emanating from the statue, growing brighter with each moment, filling the room, and enveloping you.

This light is the divine feminine power of Isis. Allow this energy to flow through you, from the top of your head, down your spine, and to your feet. As it moves, feel it awakening your intuition, strengthening your resolve, and sparking your creativity.

See yourself absorbing Isis's qualities – her nurturing nature, her wisdom, her resilience. Feel a deep connection with the divine feminine within you, awakening, and ready to aid in your manifestation journey.

Stay in this state for as long as you feel comfortable. When you're ready, gently bring your awareness back to your physical surroundings. Take a few deep breaths, open your eyes, and come back to the present moment.

Remember, this feminine energy you've now connected with is always within you. Like Isis, you possess the power to create, to heal, to nurture.

Embrace this energy as you continue your journey of manifestation, creating the life you desire, much like Isis did in the ancient Egyptian myths.

The power of the divine feminine and the energy of Isis is not an external force to be invoked; it is a potent power within each of us. By acknowledging this power, we pave the way to a more balanced and harmonious way of manifesting our deepest desires and highest aspirations. Let the wisdom and power of Isis guide you on this journey of creation.

Chapter 14: Embodying Goddess Isis

The journey to mastering the art of manifestation is not a linear process, but a dynamic, living practice that calls for deep introspection and self-evolution. One of the profound ways to enhance this process is by embodying the qualities of the deity we have been exploring so far, Isis. As we immerse ourselves in her divine essence, we can learn to harness her energies in our day-to-day life, enhancing our power to manifest.

Isis, as we know, is a goddess of immense strength and magic, a symbol of resilience, nurturing, and creation. Her legends speak of her love, devotion, and determination. Each of these qualities has a profound lesson to teach us about manifestation, helping us evolve and align ourselves with the energy of creation.

Embodying Isis involves embracing her qualities and integrating them into our consciousness and life. It means learning from her wisdom, her actions, and her resolve. This process isn't about trying to become someone else; it's about recognizing the divine potential within us and bringing it forth in our lives.

Isis as a Symbol of Strength and Resilience

Isis' strength and resilience are legendary. Despite the numerous obstacles and tragedies she faced, she never faltered. She faced every difficulty head-on, using her inner strength and wisdom to overcome them. Isis teaches us that resilience is not merely about survival but about growing and thriving amidst challenges.

Isis's strength is an essential quality to imbibe for successful manifestation. It is natural to face hurdles in our journey, to doubt ourselves, to fear failure. However, if we can learn to adopt Isis's unwavering strength and resilience, we can navigate these hurdles with confidence, using them as stepping stones towards our goals.

To embody Isis's strength, practice standing firm in the face of adversity. When you encounter challenges, remind yourself of Isis's resilience. Visualize her strength filling you, enabling you to overcome your obstacles.

Isis as a Symbol of Nurturing and Creation

Isis is often depicted nursing her son, Horus, symbolizing her role as a nurturer. As a goddess of magic and a patroness of nature, Isis also represents the nurturing aspect of creation. She shows us the importance of tending to our desires, nurturing them like seeds, for them to grow and manifest in our lives.

To embody this nurturing energy, care for your intentions and goals as you would a precious child. Nurture your dreams with positive thoughts, care, and perseverance. Give them the love and attention they need to grow and become your reality.

Isis as a Symbol of Love and Devotion

Isis's love for her husband Osiris was so profound that she traversed the Underworld and used her magic to resurrect him. Her devotion did not waver, even in the face of unimaginable grief. Love and devotion, in the context of manifestation, imply a deep, unwavering belief in our goals and desires.

To embody Isis's love and devotion, cultivate a deep passion for your dreams. Develop a resolute belief in your ability to achieve them. Hold onto this belief, even when your journey gets difficult. Let this unwavering belief fuel your manifestation process.

Isis as a Symbol of Wisdom and Magic

Isis was a goddess of magic and wisdom. Her magical abilities were tied to her deep wisdom about life, death, and creation. Embodying Isis's wisdom and magic means tuning into our inner wisdom, listening to our intuition, and trusting in the natural magic of the universe.

Practice tuning into your intuition regularly. Trust that you have the wisdom to make the right decisions. Believe in the magic that surrounds you, the magic of synchronicities, signs from the universe, and the power of your intentions.

Guided Meditation for Invoking Isis Within

Now that we understand the qualities of Isis and how they apply to manifestation, we can practice invoking these energies within us through a guided meditation.

Find a quiet space where you won't be disturbed and sit comfortably. Close your eyes and take a few deep breaths, grounding yourself in the present moment.

Visualize the image of Isis, resplendent in her robes, a symbol of strength, resilience, nurturing, love, and magic. As you breathe in, imagine her energy flowing into you, filling you with her divine essence. As you breathe out, let go of any doubts or fears, surrendering them to Isis.

With each breath, feel her strength and resilience filling you, enabling you to face any obstacle in your path. Feel her nurturing energy, teaching you how to tenderly care for your dreams and desires. Feel her love and devotion, igniting a resolute belief in your dreams. Finally, feel her wisdom and magic, attuning you to your intuition and the magic of the universe.

Spend a few moments soaking in this energy, feeling it become a part of you. When you're ready, gently bring yourself back to your physical surroundings and open your eyes.

Practice this meditation regularly to embody Isis's energies. As you continue to integrate her qualities into your life, you'll find yourself aligning more with the energy of creation, thus enhancing your manifestation abilities.

Embodying Isis is a transformative journey, one that not only enhances our manifestation abilities but also leads to profound self-growth. As we bring forth the qualities of Isis within us, we evolve and align ourselves with the divine, becoming more empowered creators of our reality.

Chapter 15: Goddess Isis and Dreams

The realm of dreams has always been shrouded in mystery and enigma. Dreams can be fantastical and symbolic, representing a myriad of hidden emotions, thoughts, and insights that our conscious mind might overlook. This chapter explores the fascinating relationship between the goddess Isis and dreams and how dreams can serve as a powerful tool for manifestation.

Isis, the ancient Egyptian goddess, is a figure of magic, healing, and transformation. But there is an aspect of her character less discussed but equally important—her association with dreams. Isis, as the "Lady of Words of Power," could harness the potential of dreams to bring forth the desired reality, helping us understand that dreams can be instrumental in the process of manifestation.

In many ways, our dreams are manifestations themselves. They are the embodiment of our subconscious thoughts, emotions, and desires. When we sleep, our conscious mind relinquishes control, and the subconscious mind takes over, weaving stories and scenarios that may often seem disconnected from our waking reality but carry within them profound symbolism and meaning.

The Ancient Egyptians held dreams in high regard. They saw dreams as messages from the gods and the divine realm, providing guidance, warnings, and revelations. Dream interpreters, or 'Masters of the Secret Things', were esteemed in the society, revealing the hidden meanings and guiding individuals based on the wisdom of the dreams.

Isis herself was known to appear in dreams, offering her wisdom and guidance. She is the great enchantress, a magician who could make things manifest through her magical words. In the same way, our dreams can serve as our own words of power, enabling us to tap into the depths of our subconscious and bring forth into reality what we truly desire.

Engaging with your dreams consciously allows you to communicate with your subconscious mind, the place where many of our deeply held beliefs and blocks reside. Uncovering and understanding these can lead to transformative healing and a clearer path to manifestation.

Now, let's delve into the meditative process that will assist you in activating the power of dreams, inspired by Isis's wisdom.

Dream Meditation for Manifestation

This meditation is best performed just before sleep, as it allows you to transition smoothly from a state of relaxation into the dream state. It is essential to create a serene and peaceful environment before you begin.

Preparation: Begin by making your sleeping area comfortable and calming. You might light some incense or use essential oils to create a soothing atmosphere. Lavender and chamomile can be particularly effective in promoting relaxation.

Relaxation: Sit comfortably on your bed and close your eyes. Take a few deep breaths, inhaling peace and tranquility, and exhaling any stress or tension. Feel your body becoming lighter and more relaxed with each breath.

Invocation: In your mind's eye, envision the figure of Isis. See her radiant figure enveloped in the soft glow of moonlight. Invoke her presence by saying, "Goddess Isis, Lady of Words of Power, guide me through the realm of dreams."

Setting Intentions: Speak to Isis about your desire for manifestation. Whether it's a particular goal or a personal transformation, articulate your intention clearly. Trust that Isis hears your words.

Entering the Dream State: As you feel the presence of Isis around you, imagine yourself standing at the edge of a vast, dreamy landscape. Ask Isis to guide you through this realm, to help you understand the messages that come forth, and harness their power for manifestation.

Integration: Imagine your dream landscape blending with your reality, symbolizing the manifestation of your intentions.

Gratitude: Show your appreciation to Isis for her guidance, and gently pull your awareness back to your physical surroundings. Drift to sleep with the assurance that your dreams will provide guidance on your path to manifestation.

This dream meditation sets the stage for proactive dreaming. Keeping a dream journal can be highly beneficial in this practice. Write down your dreams immediately upon waking, and over time, observe patterns, recurring symbols, or messages. These are the "words of power" that your subconscious mind is communicating to you.

Understanding dreams is a personal journey as each symbol may hold different meanings for different individuals. Listen to your intuition while deciphering your dreams. If a particular symbol evokes a specific feeling or memory, pay attention to it.

Remember, the path of manifestation is not always straightforward. Your dreams may bring to light fears or blocks that you need to address to manifest your desires effectively. This is part of the process, a part that Isis, the great healer, assists you with.

The realm of dreams is a magical, powerful space. It's where reality bends and the laws of the physical world do not apply. Isis, as your guide in this realm, can help you tap into this power, enabling you to not only explore your deepest self but also manifest your true desires.

In the words of the ancient Egyptians, "A dream which has not been interpreted is like a letter which has not been read." So, embark on this dream journey, explore your subconscious "letters," and allow the wisdom of Isis to guide you towards powerful manifestation.

Chapter 16: Working with Crystals

Working with crystals is an age-old practice that has deep roots in many cultures. Ancient Egyptians held a deep reverence for these earthly treasures, and they held an integral place in their spiritual and practical life. Isis, as one of the most venerated deities of ancient Egypt, has particular associations with certain crystals which can serve as powerful tools in your manifestation journey. In this chapter, we will explore the crystals connected to Isis, understand their properties, and learn how they can amplify our manifestation efforts. Finally, we will guide you through a meditation for crystal charging and programming.

Firstly, it's essential to comprehend why crystals hold such a significant role in spiritual practices. Crystals, in their most fundamental sense, are pieces of the Earth. They are born from intense heat and pressure, transforming into complex, geometrically perfect structures over millions of years. As a result, each crystal vibrates with a unique energy frequency that can be harnessed to balance energies, aid healing, amplify intention, and manifest desires. This synergistic interaction between humans and crystals is what makes them powerful spiritual tools.

Let's delve into the crystals closely associated with the goddess Isis, their properties, and how they can enhance our manifestation efforts:

Lapis Lazuli: Revered as a stone of royalty and spirituality, Lapis Lazuli was extensively used in ancient Egypt. It resonates with the energy of Isis, signifying wisdom, truth, and enlightenment. The deep blue color of the stone is reminiscent of the night sky, which links it to Isis's celestial aspect. When you seek wisdom or knowledge in your manifestation journey, or when your goals align with intellectual pursuits or communication, Lapis Lazuli is your crystal ally.

Carnelian: Carnelian is another stone deeply linked to ancient Egypt. Its vibrant, life-affirming colors resonate with Isis's role as a life-giver and nurturer. It is a stone of creativity, courage, and vitality. If your manifestation goals are related to creativity, passion, or courage, working with Carnelian can be extremely beneficial.

Moonstone: As a goddess closely tied to lunar energies, Isis has a special connection with the Moonstone. It is a stone of intuition, emotional balance, and new beginnings. For manifestations that involve transitions, emotional healing, or tapping into your intuition, the Moonstone is a fitting choice.

Now, let's explore a meditation for charging and programming these crystals, or any others that you feel drawn to work with.

Before beginning, cleanse your chosen crystal. This can be done by running it under cold water, leaving it in the moonlight, or using a cleansing incense or sound. Cleansing helps to remove any lingering energies, leaving your crystal ready to accept your intention.

Crystal Charging and Programming Meditation

Find a quiet, peaceful space where you will not be disturbed. Sit comfortably, holding your chosen crystal in your left hand, as this is the hand typically associated with receiving energy.

Close your eyes and take a moment to ground yourself. Visualize roots extending from your feet, anchoring you firmly to the Earth. Take a few deep breaths, inhaling peace and calm, exhaling any tension or negativity.

Once you feel grounded, visualize a soft, warm light emanating from your heart center. Feel this light filled with your intention for manifestation. What do you wish to manifest? Picture it in as much detail as possible. Feel the emotions associated with achieving this desire. Imbue the light from your heart with these emotions.

Now, imagine this light, dense with your intention, flowing from your heart, down your arm, and into the crystal in your hand. Picture your crystal soaking up this light, its own glow becoming brighter and pulsating in sync with your heartbeat.

Recite, "Dear Isis, guide me as I program this crystal with my intention. Let its vibration resonate with my desires, amplifying them out into the Universe. Guide me to take inspired action and trust in the unfolding process. So mote it be."

Stay in this state for a few more moments, feeling the energy exchange between you and your crystal. When you're ready, open your eyes.

After the meditation, keep the crystal close by. It will serve as a tangible reminder of your goals and a conduit for the manifestation energy you have programmed into it.

In this chapter, we have connected the wisdom of Isis with the earthly power of crystals. Each crystal carries its own unique frequency, and when combined with your intention, it can prove to be a potent tool for manifestation. Remember, your journey with crystals should be personal and intuitive. Let your intuition guide you in choosing your crystal allies, and may Isis's wisdom accompany you on this journey towards manifesting your desires.

Chapter 17: Healing with Goddess Isis

Manifestation isn't solely about achieving material prosperity or cultivating desirable relationships. An integral part of this process is the manifestation of inner well-being and wholeness – the healing of our spiritual, emotional, and physical selves.

In the pantheon of ancient Egyptian deities, Isis holds a significant place as the goddess of life, health, wisdom, and healing. In her lore, Isis is remembered for her potent healing powers, which even brought her husband Osiris back to life. Isis's energy offers the profound essence of healing, restoration, and rejuvenation that we can channel in our lives to facilitate our journey toward self-healing and inner growth.

The journey of self-healing is like the unfolding of a lotus. As we delve deeper into our own consciousness, layer by layer, we unveil our true essence, mirroring the journey of Isis who assembled the fragmented pieces of Osiris. It's about acknowledging our traumas, fears, and pains and transforming them into wisdom and strength. It's about finding the light in our shadow, mirroring the duality inherent in Isis as the goddess of both life and death.

The following meditation is designed to facilitate this deep healing process, incorporating the wisdom and energy of Isis. It's not only a journey toward healing but also a journey toward the essence of who you truly are.

Isis Healing Meditation:

Find a quiet, comfortable place where you won't be disturbed. Make sure your body is relaxed, whether you choose to sit or lie down. Begin by taking deep, slow breaths, inhaling through your nose and exhaling through your mouth. Allow yourself to release any tension in your body with each exhale.

Visualize yourself standing on the banks of the River Nile, under the silver light of the moon. The river flows calmly, mirroring the energy of healing that is about to manifest. As you stand there, you see a lotus flower floating towards you. Pick it up and hold it in your hands. It represents your heart, filled with both known and unknown pains, fears, and traumas.

Now, see the goddess Isis emerging from the radiant moonlight, walking toward you. She is an epitome of grace, strength, and wisdom. As she stands before you, she radiates an energy that feels like a warm, loving embrace.

Tell Isis about your pains, your fears, and your traumas. Speak to her about your desire for healing and the need for her divine intervention. As you do so, envision those feelings seeping out from the lotus flower you hold, being replaced by radiant light.

Isis, with her deep, compassionate gaze, acknowledges your pain. She reaches out and gently places her hand over the lotus flower. As she whispers ancient healing words, a soft golden glow emanates from her hand, seeping into the lotus, transforming the radiating light into a brilliant golden hue.

This golden light is the light of healing, wisdom, and renewal. It symbolizes Isis's powerful healing energy. As you hold the glowing lotus close to your heart, imagine this healing energy seeping into your being, illuminating every cell of your body, every corner of your heart, every fragment of your soul.

Feel this energy healing your wounds, soothing your pains, and mending your heart. Let it transform your fears into courage, your pains into wisdom, and your traumas into strength. Let this energy rejuvenate your being, as Osiris was revived, restoring your wholeness and well-being.

Take a few more moments in the presence of Isis, absorbing her healing energy, feeling lighter, brighter, and healed. Thank Isis for her divine intervention, and when you're ready, bid her farewell. Watch as she walks back into the moonlight, merging with it.

Now, come back to the riverbank, holding the golden lotus, a symbol of your healed self. Slowly, release the lotus back into the Nile, releasing your healed self into the universe.

Gradually bring your awareness back to the room you're in. Feel the surface beneath you, listen to the sounds around you. Wiggle your fingers and toes, stretch your body, and when you're ready, gently open your eyes.

Remember, healing is a journey, not a destination. It takes time, patience, and compassionate understanding towards yourself. Like Isis, you possess the ability to heal, grow, and transform. So, allow the healing process to unfold naturally, let it guide you towards your inner growth, and trust in the wisdom and strength that it cultivates within you. By integrating the energy of Isis in our healing journey, we not only manifest a healthier, whole self, but we also contribute to the manifestation of a healthier, whole universe.

Chapter 18: Goddess Isis and Prosperity

In our journey through the lens of ancient Egyptian wisdom and Isis's teachings, we have discovered many layers of manifestation, all with the potential to significantly impact our lives. We have explored the power of thought, sacred symbols, cycles of life, and even lunar energy. In this chapter, we are going to delve into a concept that is usually at the forefront of manifestation for many people - Prosperity.

Isis, as the Goddess of life, magic, and fertility, also played an essential role in the aspect of abundance and prosperity. To the ancient Egyptians, she was a symbol of bountifulness and was often invoked to bless the lands and ensure a fruitful harvest. Isis's wisdom teaches us that abundance is not merely a state of having more; it is an attitude and a way of life.

We live in an abundant universe. However, many of us often perceive lack due to various limiting beliefs and societal constructs. The art of manifestation and Isis's teachings can help us transcend these limitations and align with the energy of prosperity.

Isis and the Concept of Prosperity

To truly understand prosperity in the context of Isis's teachings, we must first comprehend the ancient Egyptian perception of wealth. Unlike the modern perspective, where wealth is often associated only with material gain, the ancient Egyptians had a more holistic view. They believed that abundance transcended the physical realm and included health, joy, love, and spiritual fulfillment. Isis, as a universal goddess, encompassed all these aspects, embodying the ideal of a prosperous life.

The ancient Egyptians didn't separate their spiritual lives from their everyday existence. They perceived the divine in everything around them, from the sun that warmed their lands to the Nile that nourished their crops. They understood that the universe was abundant, and the energy of abundance was always available to them. This philosophy is perfectly encapsulated in Isis, whose roles ranged from a nurturing mother, a wise healer, a powerful magician, to a goddess of abundance.

Aligning with the Energy of Abundance

In the realm of manifestation, alignment is everything. You attract not what you want, but who you are. Therefore, to manifest prosperity, you need to align with the energy of abundance.

Isis teaches us that abundance is our natural state. When we connect with the energy of Isis, we attune ourselves to the frequency of abundance, and we start attracting more of it into our lives.

One effective way to align with this energy is through gratitude. The practice of gratitude is a powerful magnet for abundance. When we are grateful for what we already have, we send a message to the universe that we appreciate its gifts, and in response, the universe brings more gifts our way. Remember, Isis is also the Goddess of gratitude. She was always thankful for her blessings, which were reflected in the love and devotion of her followers.

Prosperity Meditation

To solidify your alignment with the energy of abundance, it's beneficial to engage in a guided prosperity meditation. This meditation will serve as a vessel for you to connect deeper with Isis's energy and the abundant nature of the universe.

Start by finding a quiet space where you won't be disturbed. Sit comfortably, close your eyes, and take a few deep breaths to ground yourself. Visualize a warm, golden light emanating from your heart center, filling your entire being.

Now, imagine Isis standing before you, dressed in a gown of brilliant gold, her face radiating with kindness and wisdom. In her hands, she holds an Ankh, the symbol of eternal life and abundance. Feel her energy of abundance flowing towards you, saturating every cell of your body with the essence of prosperity.

Silently say to yourself, "I am open to receive the abundance of the universe." Feel your energy field expanding and aligning with the frequency of abundance. Imagine all your needs and desires being fulfilled effortlessly. Hold this feeling as long as you can, and when you're ready, slowly open your eyes.

This meditation is not a one-time activity but a continuous process. The more you engage with it, the more you will attune yourself with the energy of abundance.

Living a Prosperous Life

Living a prosperous life means more than just having a large bank account. It's about experiencing the richness of life in all its forms - love, joy, health, fulfillment, and yes, even material wealth. Isis's teachings inspire us to seek a balanced and holistic approach to prosperity.

It's crucial to remember that the universe is inherently abundant. There is enough for everyone. By tapping into the energy of Isis, you're not taking away from anyone else. Instead, you're aligning with the natural state of the universe - a state of endless possibilities and limitless abundance.

When you start living from a place of abundance, you'll notice significant changes in your life. You'll find more opportunities coming your way, your relationships will thrive, and you'll experience a sense of peace and satisfaction that stems from knowing you are part of an abundant universe.

Isis, the Goddess of abundance, teaches us that prosperity is our birthright. By connecting with her energy, practicing gratitude, and aligning ourselves with the abundant nature of the universe, we can manifest a prosperous life in all its forms. As we continue our journey, remember that the art of manifestation is a journey, not a destination. Each step brings us closer to our true essence, that of limitless potential and boundless abundance.

Chapter 19: Goddess Isis and Love

Among the many roles that the ancient Egyptian goddess Isis played, she was also revered as a deity of love, passion, and fertility. Her deep love for her husband Osiris, and her relentless pursuit to revive him after his death, is an inspiring testament to the strength and power of her love. In her, we see a symbol of enduring devotion, unconditional love, and the ability to heal and restore. As we delve into this chapter, we will learn how Isis's energy can help in manifesting love and relationships.

In the vastness of the cosmos, Isis is a symbol of divine feminine energy, capable of immense love and nurturing. She embodies qualities like compassion, understanding, patience, and harmony—qualities that form the bedrock of any successful and loving relationship. By aligning ourselves with Isis's energy, we can harness these qualities in our lives and manifest the kind of love and relationship we yearn for.

Before we delve deeper, it's important to remember that love, in the context of this chapter, doesn't strictly refer to romantic love. While Isis can certainly guide us in attracting a romantic partner, her energy also aids in fostering familial love, strengthening friendships, and enhancing self-love.

First, let's focus on self-love.

Self-Love and Goddess Isis

The ancient Egyptians held the belief that the soul, or "ka," resided in the heart. It was the center of life-force and consciousness. To love oneself, therefore, was to nourish the soul. The journey of manifestation begins within, and self-love forms its foundation. Without a strong base of self-love, the energy we emit may align with lower frequencies, making it challenging to manifest love externally.

Isis, being a nurturing mother figure, showers unconditional love upon her devotees, and teaches us the importance of extending that same love to ourselves. Let's explore a guided meditation to foster self-love:

Begin by finding a quiet, comfortable space where you won't be disturbed. Close your eyes and take a few deep breaths, allowing your body to relax. Visualize yourself standing before Isis on the banks of the Nile under the moonlight. See her compassionate eyes and feel her nurturing energy. She reaches out, placing her hand over your heart. You feel a warm, gentle energy entering you—this is Isis's love for you. Allow it to fill you, healing any hurts and filling any voids within you. Spend a few moments in this space, basking in Isis's love. When you're ready, thank Isis and bring your awareness back to your surroundings. Practice this meditation daily to foster a deep sense of self-love.

Manifesting Love in Relationships

When it comes to manifesting love in relationships, whether it be a romantic partnership, a familial bond, or a friendship, Isis's energy can guide us towards creating healthy, loving connections.

In Isis's story, we witness her devotion to her husband Osiris and her dedication to restore him to life. From this, we can glean the importance of commitment, resilience, and the healing power of love in relationships. Aligning with Isis's energy in our quest for love means nurturing these qualities within ourselves.

Here's a meditation to aid you in attracting love and strengthening relationships:

Once again, find a quiet space where you won't be disturbed. Close your eyes and take deep, calming breaths. Visualize a beautiful garden bathed in the soft, warm light of the setting sun. Isis appears before you, her presence radiating love and warmth. Share with her your desires for love—be it a romantic partner, a deeper bond with family, or a strengthened friendship. Feel her listen to your words, her energy responding with understanding and compassion.

Isis then takes a golden ankh, the symbol of life, and touches your heart with it. You feel a surge of warmth, of love, of possibility. She is imparting her blessing upon you, aligning your energy with the love you seek. Spend some time in this feeling, letting it seep into the very core of your being.

When you're ready, thank Isis and slowly bring your awareness back to your physical surroundings. Continue this practice as part of your daily routine, truly believing in the process of manifestation.

Love is a potent force of connection and healing. Isis, as a deity of love, offers her aid to those seeking to manifest love in its various forms. Through these meditations and a consistent practice of aligning ourselves with Isis's energy, we can invite love into our lives. Remember, the process of manifestation is a journey, and like Isis's journey to revive Osiris, it may require patience, dedication, and unwavering belief.

As we continue to harness the divine energy of Isis, we enrich our potential to manifest love, healing, and transformation in our lives, opening our hearts to the infinite possibilities of the universe.

Chapter 20: Final Thoughts and Continuing Practice

Over the course of our exploration into the world of Isis and the art of manifestation, we've journeyed through ancient wisdom, tapped into the power of symbols and affirmations, and utilized meditative practices to hone our manifestation abilities. As we close this transformative period of study and growth, it's essential to remember that the path of manifestation is a lifelong journey. Like the cycle of birth, death, and rebirth that Isis so powerfully represents, our manifestation practice is a perpetual process of creation, dissolution, and recreation.

Let's begin by recapping key concepts we've learned throughout this journey. We started with an introduction to Isis, the ancient Egyptian goddess of magic, motherhood, healing, and rebirth. Isis, as we discovered, is not just a mythical figure but a symbol of the inherent creative power within each one of us.

Manifestation, in its simplest terms, is the act of bringing our thoughts, ideas, and desires into tangible existence. It's about consciously creating our reality rather than passively experiencing it. Manifestation is more than just wishful thinking— it's a process that requires clarity of intention, positive mental conditioning, focused energy, and an unwavering belief in the possibility of your vision.

We explored the role of Isis in manifestation, harnessing the power of thought, and the significance of sacred symbols and amulets. We learned how to craft powerful affirmations that align with our desires and help shift our reality. We tapped into the wisdom of natural cycles, the power of visualization, and the potent energies of the natural world.

As we embodied Isis's wisdom, we learned to understand and harness lunar energy, the divine feminine, and the wisdom of dreams. We worked with crystals, invoked spiritual healing, and harnessed Isis's energy for prosperity and love. Each step of this journey provided us with a set of tools and practices to support our manifestation endeavors.

Continuing this practice requires integrating what we've learned into our daily lives. Manifestation isn't a one-time event—it's a way of living that involves continual alignment with our intentions, staying open to opportunities, and releasing resistance.

Maintain a Daily Meditation Practice

Meditation is a vital tool for manifestation. It helps us clear mental clutter, focus our intentions, and align our energy with the universe. Daily meditation allows us to connect with the energy of Isis, harnessing her wisdom and power. In our final meditation, let's combine all the elements we've learned.

Final Meditation

Begin by finding a quiet, comfortable space where you won't be disturbed. Sit or lie down in a relaxed position, close your eyes, and take several deep, cleansing breaths.

Visualize the radiant figure of Isis before you, her wings spread wide, her presence both powerful and comforting. Feel her divine energy flowing towards you, enveloping you in a soft, nurturing glow.

Invoke the power of your sacred symbols, affirmations, and crystals. Feel the energy of the moon and nature surrounding you. Recall your intentions, visualizing them as seeds sprouting in a fertile field, growing and blossoming under the loving gaze of Isis.

Feel the divine feminine energy within you. Connect with the cycles of life, the wisdom of dreams, and the abundance of prosperity and love. See your dreams manifesting in the physical realm, your desires unfolding beautifully in your life.

Thank the goddess Isis for her guidance, support, and nurturing energy. Feel a deep sense of gratitude for everything you've learned and manifested. Take several deep breaths and slowly bring your awareness back to your physical surroundings.

Embody Goddess Isis Daily

Embodying the qualities of Isis means living with wisdom, compassion, strength, and creativity. Tap into the power of Isis when faced with challenges or decisions. Use her wisdom to guide you and her strength to empower you.

Keep a Dream Journal

Your dreams are a powerful tool for manifestation. They can provide insights, answer questions, and guide you towards your desires. Keeping a dream journal helps you remember and interpret your dreams, enabling you to harness their wisdom for manifestation.

Practice Gratitude

Gratitude is a powerful vibration that aligns us with abundance. Practicing daily gratitude can dramatically shift your energy and attract more of what you want into your life.

Believe in Your Power

Above all, believe in your power to manifest. Know that like Isis, you are a divine being capable of creating your reality. Your thoughts, intentions, and actions have the power to transform your life.

Remember, manifestation is a journey, not a destination. Be patient, trust the process, and most importantly, enjoy the journey. May the wisdom of Isis guide you, her power inspire you, and her love nurture you on your path of manifestation. You are a powerful creator, capable of manifesting your deepest desires and living a life of purpose, abundance, and joy. Blessings on your continued journey.

Made in the USA
Middletown, DE
16 October 2023